Stay Gold

Stay Gold

An inspiration to those who have lost someone.

Linda MacDonald

ISBN: 0692435050
ISBN 13: 9780692435052

Acknowledgements

FIRST I MUST thank Tina Karosas for giving me the inspiration to write this book. You not only inspired me, you guided and helped me get this book started. Without you it may have never come to fruition.

To Charlie Orlando, for your tremendous editing support and guidance to the books final end. Thank you for helping me get this book to where it is today.

To all of my friends who are mentioned in this book. Thank you for your love, for your support, and for believing in these unexplainable events that have touched us all.

To my awesome and brave daughters, Jaclyn and Meghan; you have shown me what strength is. You may have thought I was being strong through this unimaginable time, but it was both of you who gave me the strength I needed.

Most of all, a special thank you to my husband Michael. You are truly an amazing husband and a wonderful father to our children. Thank you from the bottom of my heart, for your love, your support, and for always being by my side.

Introduction

My husband, Michael, and I have been married for twenty-two years and raised three children: Ryan, twenty; Jaclyn, seventeen; and Meghan, fifteen. We met at Strawbridge & Clothier department store in Wilmington, Delaware. Michael was the department manager of housewares, and I was the manager of the linen department. We were married two years after we met, and we lived in a townhouse in Bear, Delaware, where Ryan and Jaclyn were born. After living there three years, it was time for a bigger home. We decided to leave Delaware and move to Pennsylvania. At this point, I would like to mention that Michael had lived outside of Philadelphia his whole life. Michael's father, Jack, had turned him into a huge, devout, and loyal Philadelphia Eagles fan at an early age. Michael had passed this on to our son, Ryan.

My friend Stefanie lived in Florida, and I would visit her about once a year with Ryan. She had a son his age. Michael came with me once and told Stefanie how lucky she was to live in such a beautiful place. After our visit, I suggested we could move there. The kids were only two, four, and six years old then. I said I would love a change of lifestyle, and the kids were at a perfect age for such a move. So we did it and have loved everything about living in Florida.

Early on we decided to send the kids to Catholic schools, if we could afford to do so. I also wanted to be a stay-at-home mom. Lucky for us, we were able to do both. Even when we moved to Florida, we were able to get Ryan and Jaclyn into a Catholic school, despite it being the middle of a school year. Meghan was still home with me until she was of age for pre-K. It wasn't that we were particularly devout Catholics, but Michael had gone to Catholic schools, and we thought it would be good for our kids too.

As parents, that's all we can do: what we think is the best for our kids. We choose the schools they go to; we stay home with them if we can, giving up on our career plans. We try to give them good values and make sure they surround themselves with good friends. We try to ensure they eat the right foods. We don't let them watch too much television or spend too much time on a computer, and we make sure they get a good night's sleep. We try to warn them about certain strangers and make sure they are home before dark. Why? Because no parent wants to deal with the unthinkable: the loss of a child.

On December 15, 2014, the unthinkable happened to Michael and me. Our twenty-year-old son passed away. There are no words to describe the emotions that engulf a parent when you learn your child is gone. But that's not what this book is about. Not entirely. It's about what transpired during the six weeks after Ryan was gone, starting the day he passed away.

I've never thought of myself as being particularly spiritual or one who believes in signs or destiny. But what happened to me, my family, and my friends during those weeks defies logical explanation. There are witnesses to and proof of everything that happened to us. And it was the power of these incidents that got me through the darkest and saddest days of my life.

Then my friend Tina came to me and suggested I write a book. These moments needed to be shared because, she believed, our story could truly help others. It was at that moment I knew that I would do it. I'm not a writer, but I am a mom who lost my child. If this little book can help another parent or anyone who has lost someone, then I have accomplished a meaningful purpose.

Foreword

*W*AKING UP THIS *morning to a knock on the door from the police,
telling us that you had died, was a pause on life. To never forget
how fragile life is. I never would have thought I would have lost
not only my brother but my best friend. It's believed you live
for a purpose, and you had obviously fulfilled that purpose, and
it was your time to go. You will still forever be my best friend,
no matter what. As much pain and suffering as it will take to
overcome this, I know you are watching over us and letting us
know everything will be okay. All I wish for you is to be at peace
with God and to let us know you're okay. I love you more than
the world will ever know. Rest in peace, Ryan. God gained.*

Jaclyn MacDonald
Seventeen years old
December 15, 2014
Instagram

Monday, December 15

Lake Worth, Florida

WITHIN HOURS AFTER we were first notified that Ryan was gone, my husband and I received a telephone call. It was the Florida Lions Eye Bank informing us that Ryan was an organ donor and they wanted permission to take his eyes. Unfortunately, because he had lost so much blood, no other organs could be transplanted. That was one of the most unimaginable circumstances I ever thought that I would be in: trying to begin to comprehend that my son was gone and then having to make such a heart-wrenching decision.

I had always emphasized the importance of being an organ donor to my kids, because if any of them needed an organ, I would gratefully accept it from someone else's loss. Never did I ever imagine the loss would be mine, and one of my children would be the donor.

My heart and mind were in a whirlwind, trying to grasp this unthinkable reality. In my heart I knew it was the right thing to do, yet it was still somehow difficult to give that permission. But we did. Later that day we got the call that Ryan's eyes had helped not just one but two people. At that moment, I felt a little sense of pride that my son had started his journey of charity.

On the night of December 15, after my friends had left, I was finally alone. I went out back and sat on the wicker love seat Ryan always sat on, and I cried. Not that I hadn't cried—and screamed—several times, all day long, but at last I was alone and could really let myself go.

I looked up at the stars and kept saying, "Oh, Ryan… oh, Ryan…oh, Ryan." As I looked to the sky, I noticed this huge and unusually bright constellation. I went silent and stared at it through my red, swollen, and teary eyes. In my moment of silence, as I stared heavenward, something came to me: Was the constellation I was looking at Orion?

I must say, I do not know a lot about astronomy, so I wasn't sure if what I was seeing was really Orion. So I ran into the house to get my husband. Then I ran to my neighbors, who had been with me all day, to ask them to come and see. My neighbor Danielle loves to look things up on Google, so I had her Google *Orion* to make sure that was what we were all staring at. She confirmed it was indeed Orion, pronounced just like "Oh, Ryan." We all stood there in silence, just staring into the sky.

How could this be? First of all, I had never sat on that love seat before, because Ryan was always sitting there. If I had sat in the seat I normally took, I would not have been able to see the constellation. Secondly, how did the constellation named Orion pop into my head? On any other day, if you had asked me about stars or constellations, the only ones I could have named were the Big Dipper and the Little Dipper.

Then someone said, "It's a sign from him." Whether it was a sign that he was okay or that he was watching over us, it didn't matter to me, because in my heart I knew it was a sign from my son.

Orion, the hunter, is the most famous seasonal constellation and is best seen during the winter. Orion looks very much like a person. First, you can spot Orion's belt, three stars in a row. Two other stars mark his shoulders, and two more form his legs—one of which is among the brightest stars in the sky.[1]

After learning all these facts, it only made me surer that this was a sign from Ryan.

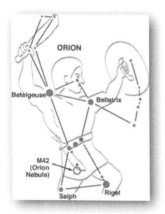
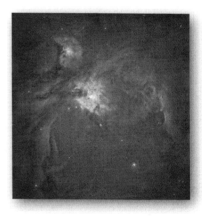

In another house, miles away, my friend Joan was feeling my grief and staring at the same night sky as I was. Her heart ached for me, as a friend and as a mother herself, trying to imagine the depth of my loss. She felt compelled to do something, anything, to commemorate Ryan's memory and to ease my broken heart. She walked into her house and, with the power of the Internet, was able to buy the naming rights to a star that night.

The star will forever reside in the heavens, and it is now called Ryan Patrick MacDonald. The star was first located in the sky on December 6, 2014, which was Ryan's twentieth birthday. The card from the International Star Registry reads, "Know that you can look at the stars and know Ryan is always with you."

I was unaware my friend had done this until I received the star documents and framed registration two days later. Again, it was one of those moments in which I could only stare in disbelief. Was I stunned because she bought this commemoration or because I'd learned she had never done this before? Or was it the fact she had been staring into the sky that night, too? And then there was the fact that the star was discovered on his birthday. When we put all the pieces together, all we could come up with was that it could only be a sign from Ryan. Not only did this console my family, but when I told Joan my story of Orion, it consoled her that somehow Ryan had reached out to her, too, to motivate her to do something so meaningful.

Tuesday, December 16

MY FEELINGS UPON waking up the day after hearing that my son was gone were beyond description. All I wanted to do was stay in bed and pretend none of it had happened. But my husband and I knew that we had to find a funeral home that day and, if possible, schedule the service before the end of the week, because the following week was Christmas. There was no way I was going to have the service that close to Christmas.

So I got out of bed, got some coffee, went out back, and sat on the love seat and started thinking, *How am I going to do this? I don't even have the strength to get dressed.* Then I started thinking, *This is going to be one of the most important things my husband and I can do to honor Ryan.* So I cleared my head of the sad thoughts, and then my mind was racing: *How do we make this service the best that it can be?*

I called my friend Patti, who had lived in West Palm Beach all her life and knew everyone in town, and asked her, "What is the best funeral home that you know of in town?" She said, "Quattlebaum."[2] I ran upstairs and told my husband that he needed to call them right away. He had checked on a couple of other funeral homes, but they

5

didn't meet our needs. I had told my husband earlier that the place had to be perfect. I wanted it to be warm and comforting, almost like our home.

Because this was so important to my husband and me, to honor Ryan in the best way possible, I found myself with newfound energy. I rushed to the shower and got dressed, and we were at Quattlebaum in an hour and a half. When we pulled up, we saw the sign: "Quattlebaum Funeral, Cremation, and Event Center." The company's motto was "Honoring memories and celebrating lives." We looked at each other and said, "Yes, that's what we are going to do. Not a memorial or funeral service, but a celebration of Ryan's life." I took a deep breath as we crossed the threshold into the main lobby. I stopped to look around and was surprised by what I saw. The room was warmly arranged; there was almost a sense of peace to it. It was beautiful, light, yet cozy with love seats and high ceilings. I wasn't sure if it was the lighting or the colors they chose to use, but it was much nicer than I had dreamed the place could be. It had the feel that I so much desired, and I knew at that moment it was the perfect place.

But it was such a painful meeting—beyond explanation. There were so many decisions to be made, and there I was, still trying to grasp the fact that my son was gone. But I pushed through. A question came up about food. I thought to myself, *We don't need food. Who would even be in the mood to eat?* But Richard, our consultant, tried to explain that this event was not going to be like a memorial or funeral service; it would be more of a *celebration*. We would serve light food and beverages—soft drinks, tea, coffee, and bottled water. So I made some additional food choices, and we moved on.

Richard took us into the Grand Room, which was off the lobby. It was a big, airy room, elegant yet warm, and again with that same cozy feeling the lobby had.

Richard asked us how many tables we would need. I looked at him again with confusion. "We are having *tables?* I thought there would be rows of chairs."

He reiterated, "Remember, we are trying to set the mood for a *celebration*, not a memorial."

It was at that point I realized the service was going to be like nothing I had ever seen before, and I took advantage of our advisor's expertise. We stood in the middle of the room. He explained that a back room was where the food and drinks would be. There was a glass partition separating it from the main room. There were high-top tables and stools, love seats and chairs with tables beside them. It was a place where people could go to step away, but with the glass wall, they could still feel they were a part of the activities in the main room. Up front were small palm trees, beautiful sconces, and two built-in televisions. He asked if we could gather up at least a hundred photographs, which could be shown on the televisions like a slide show. We agreed to bring them to him.

The place was amazing, and I was so pleased with the decisions we made. We still had a lot to do in only a short amount of time. We decided the celebration was going to be that Friday, December 19, only three days away.

Several months earlier I had decided I wanted a tattoo. It would be my first one, and I wanted to make sure it would be meaningful. Ryan's first tattoo was an American bald eagle—and we all know what that represents—holding a banner with all of our initials on it. I was overjoyed about the initials because I have always strived to have a close, loving family, and this showed me how much we meant to him. For my own tattoo, my friend Renee helped me come up with the design. Using Ryan's idea, she put my three kids' initials inside three little hearts. My seventeen-year-old daughter, Jaclyn, really wanted to get a tattoo with me and said it could be a mother-daughter thing. So we went to the tattoo parlor together and talked to the artist about what we wanted. He explained to us that clients must be eighteen to get a tattoo because he felt most kids would regret having done it when they got older. He felt that Jaclyn's tattoo didn't have enough meaning, and he was not willing to do it. I really appreciated his honesty, and I always believe things happen for a reason. Jaclyn was a little disappointed, but she still wanted me to get mine, and I did.

Instagram played a major role for us in those days. First of all, the quote from Jaclyn in the foreword was how the world found out about Ryan's passing. I wasn't sure how we were going to let people know, but shortly after she posted it, around noon, I started getting calls asking if it was true. For me, that was a perfect way to do it, and I was proud that she had the strength and courage to do it while I did not. Second, Jaclyn showed me what Ryan had on his

Instagram account as his bio, which can be a statement or a quotation and always remains on your account, by your name. Ryan's read: "I will leave an echo in this world that will last forever." She told me, "That's the tattoo I want to get, in that same spot that I couldn't get the other one."

At that moment, I knew that was the right thing to do. She would never regret a tattoo with a statement written by her brother. And by getting that tattoo, she would ensure that her brother would always be close to her heart and his words would indeed last forever. So I ran off to the bank to get a permission slip notarized, and then off she went to get the tattoo with her best friend, Alexa.

It was the evening of the sixteenth, and we had some close friends over, comforting my family and me. Grace, Alexa's mother, was one of them. She also had an older daughter, Christina, who was on her way home from the University of Florida, which was about a four-hour drive from our home. Grace always worried about the kids when they were driving home, especially at night. Christina was driving with friends, and Grace was texting one of the friends' mothers about their progress, but she quickly turned off her phone because Jaclyn and Alexa had just come in, and she was anxious to see Jaclyn's tattoo.

Grace still had her phone in her hand when we all got up to see the tattoo. As we were reading Ryan's words tattooed on Jaclyn's side, Grace's phone lit up. Grace was confused and flustered; she left the room to further investigate what had just happened.

When she came back in to explain, she said, "When my phone lit up and I looked at it, it was a picture of Ryan. And that picture had been sent, by text, to the other girl's mother." When she left the room, Grace had called that woman to confirm that she had indeed received a picture of the boy. The woman confirmed that she had and added, "Yes, and what a handsome fella he is."

Flabbergasted, Grace said she would try to explain it all later because in her mind she had no explanation for it. And there was no explaining this event; the camera roll hadn't been accessed, and no one had attached a picture to any of their texts. Days later, after I told this story to a friend, the friend said, "That was Ryan, trying to reach out to both mothers to let them know he was watching over the girls until they arrived home safely."

At that point, it was the only explanation that actually made sense. And unbeknownst to me, it was not the last sign Ryan would be sending to my friends or me.

Wednesday, December 17

WAKING UP TWO days after my son had passed brought the same dreadful feelings as had the previous day. I was lying in bed thinking of him, but then, once again, I began to think about all the things that needed to be done for his celebration. With my head spinning, and wanting so desperately to make it perfect, I had the motivation to get out of bed. That was the most important thing my husband and I could do for our son then—make it the most special celebration we could possibly arrange.

As mentioned, my husband, Michael, was born and raised outside of Philadelphia. His love for the Philadelphia Eagles is epic; some would say obsessively fanatical. He had passed this passion on to Ryan at an early age. After we moved to Florida, when Ryan was ten, my husband and Ryan made a pact to go to an Eagles game at least once a year from then on, and they did so for the next ten years. So as we decided on how we wanted to commemorate our son's life, we knew that to do it right, we would have to incorporate football, and that meant the Philadelphia Eagles.

The first thing we needed to decide was, instead of sending flowers, what charity would we like people to donate to in honor of Ryan? Michael thought it would be a good idea to call the Philadelphia Eagles office and ask what charities they sponsored. The woman in the office was very helpful and said they had a charity called the Eagles Youth Partnership (EYP), which specializes in vision care, literacy programs, and playgrounds for nearly one million at-risk children.[3] With EYP's focus on vision care, how ironic it was that Ryan's eyes were the only organ he was able to donate. So that decision was easy and done.

Michael and Ryan's first Eagles game

The next thing on the list was those pictures. Richard wanted us to put together collages that could be framed and placed around the room. I had spent years, countless hours with friends and by myself, scrapbooking my pictures. For a time, I was a creative memories consultant, a guru of putting photo memories into story form—my story, our family's story. Now it was time to do Ryan's story.

I grabbed all of my scrapbooks and started going through them and pulling out all the pictures I wanted to use. There were so many of them that I started to place them in piles by theme. Ryan as a baby, as a toddler, his first steps. All the holidays, birthdays, family gatherings, and vacations. The football teams he was on, the soccer teams, the Eagles games he had been to. I decided that was how I was going to do it. Each poster board would have a theme because I felt that would give the displays a classier look than just throwing a bunch of pictures up on a board, and each theme deserved its own special board. The memories often made me smile, but then reality would set in, and the pain was like a knife wound. Again, I had to force the grief from my mind, or I would never have been able to get anything done. Making those the best photo boards I'd ever done was my mission.

The first board I started was sports themed—about all the sports he had participated in and the teams he had been a fan of. I was able to finish only the one board. It was late and I was exhausted. One day and only one board complete. I had five more boards that I wanted to do because I wanted everyone to see Ryan the way I did. I have always been the type of person to get things done, and I usually did it on my own; I never liked asking for help. But that efficient, compulsive person was someplace else, without pain and sadness. I stared at the endless piles of photos, at an utter loss as to how to deal with them. I knew it was time to reach out to one of the many hands that had been extended toward me. I called my friend Patty S. She was a lot like me, a fellow scrapbooking fanatic. She also was Ryan's first-grade teacher's aide when we first moved to Florida. She was thrilled I called and said she would be over first thing the next morning.

That evening friends brought us dinner. Michael and I shared our plans for the celebration and how we were trying to transform the room, including a big salute to the Philadelphia Eagles. I had gathered all the Eagles paraphernalia that I had in my house: hats, banners, footballs, beads, bobble-head dolls, and jerseys in all sizes from when the kids were growing up. Patti H., one of the friends that were with us that evening, said, "That sounds wonderful! If there is anything that you guys need help with, please don't hesitate to ask."

Patti was known for her fun, themed gatherings. It was her Christmas luncheon that I had attended where I received a Christmas ornament, which, will be explained later in the book. I looked at her and said, "I think we are good, but thank you."

In the back of my mind, though, all I could think about was all those round tables in the center of that room at Quattlebaum. Richard had shown me the colors of the tablecloths, and I knew I wanted them to be green and white to go with the Eagles theme. But the green was a mint green, and that would not work. In the center of the tables would be a simple candle.

I looked at Patti again, took a deep breath, and said, "Well, as a matter of fact, there is something." I explained the situation with the tables and how plain and cold they would look. Then I said, "You and your friend Rodger are amazing with decorating and table arrangements. Is there any way you guys can help me liven up those tables?"

She said, "Absolutely. What exactly are you looking for?" I explained how I wanted everything to be white and green; maybe they could do a flower arrangement around the candle with green foliage and white flowers. Or anything they could think of to give those cold tables the warm, comforting feeling that I was striving for. She was thrilled to help, and I was thrilled I got the courage to ask for help—*again*.

The morning of the celebration, my husband had some things to drop off at Quattlebaum, and when he arrived, Patti, Rodger, Joan, and Diane were already there, doing their magic. My husband said to me later, "You will be blown away by what they have done."

Thursday, December 18

Waking up on the third day was no different from the first or second day. But I knew Patty S. was coming, so I forced myself out of bed. Again, I was doing this for Ryan, so I somehow found the inner strength to move forward.

At the beginning of December, there begins the flurry of events leading toward Christmas: parties, gift giving, mailing Christmas cards, and decorating the house. Being one who gets everything done early, I had already done all of the above. The story of my Christmas card will come later. I had attended a Christmas luncheon, at Patti H.'s house, where we did a gift exchange; some may know it as a white-elephant exchange. Each person brings a wrapped gift; all the gifts are put together. Each person draws a number, and the group picks gifts in the order of those numbers. When it's your turn, you can pick a wrapped gift from the center or take an open gift from someone else. I ended up with a pink flask, which I gave to a friend, and a small, plastic, almost cheap-looking ornament. I wasn't sure why I didn't throw it away. I didn't want to put it on my tree, so instead I put it on the windowsill above my kitchen sink.

As I was getting my coffee and trying to wake up before Patty S. came, I noticed a picture of me and Ryan when he was a toddler; it was taped to the window above the kitchen sink. I looked at it and thought, *What is that doing there?* One of my daughters must have seen it the day before, when I had all the photo albums out, and thought I would like it. The picture was so faded, and slightly blurry, that I almost took it down. But then I didn't want to hurt anyone's feelings, so I left it up. On my way back to the kitchen to get my second cup of coffee, I stopped and stared at the picture. As I was studying it, I realized that the picture was purposely set behind the Christmas ornament I had received. The ornament was an angel. Again, I had another one of those moments—the picture was a reminder of Ryan's past, when he was alive, smiling, and in my arms, and the angel ornament was a reminder of where he was now.

Patty S. arrived shortly after that. When I opened the door, there she stood, with tears in her eyes and cups of Dunkin' Donuts coffee in her hands, which she knew was my favorite. She came in and set the coffees down and gave me a huge hug. No words were said; tears were flowing.

She didn't know what to say, so I said, "There are no words needed, Patty; there's nothing to say."

She said, "I really hope that you will be able to find peace in all of this. I want you to have peace."

I replied, "I really think I am. I truly believe that Ryan is sending me signs that he is good, which in turn is giving me a sense of peace."

At that moment I decided to show her the angel with the picture behind it, and I explained how it all came to be. She looked down at the picture and the ornament for several seconds, and she then looked at me with amazement and said, "Did you see what the angel is giving you?"

I looked at the ornament again and said, "No, what?"

She said, "The angel has her arm reached out, and she is handing you a dove, which is a sign of peace."

Another one of *those* moments. We stared at each other. That was when I was sure that Ryan was my angel and that he was answering Patty's prayers and trying to send me peace. The clarity of those moments was just mind-blowing, and to share them with those that I was close to made it real. Again with newfound energy, the two of us were able to finish all five photo boards.

Angel Christmas ornament

As I have said before, I have a love for photographs. About ten years earlier, the kids' school held an auction. One of the items up for auction was a photo session with a well-known local photographer. I begged my husband to let me bid on it. I was trying to persuade him that pictures last forever, which was priceless, and the money would be going to the school. There nothing else there that I wanted more than that. He agreed, and we placed our bid. I was so nervous; so many other people were bidding on it also. I waited till there were only minutes left, and I placed my final bid. The auction closed, and I ran back to the bidding sheet to see if there were any more bids; there were not. We had won the photo session. Those pictures we took back then are my most treasured photos. They are still hanging all around our home.

The year of Ryan's death, my fiftieth birthday had been in September, and I had decided there would be no greater gift than having another family photo session. The kids were older, Ryan had moved out, and Jaclyn was preparing to leave for college; therefore, it felt like an opportune time. At this point, I must say, Ryan was not a big fan of getting his picture taken. He actually dreaded it. I always got nervous when it came time to take the Christmas card picture, because I knew it would be a slight battle. But to my surprise, when he asked me what I wanted for my birthday, I said, "I really, really want to do a family photo session like we did ten years ago," he said, "Okay, Mom, whatever you want."

My good friend and neighbor, Lisa, had three boys who were all into baseball. On one of the boys' teams was a boy fighting cancer. Lisa said the team was going to hold a fundraiser for the family at the baseball field, and anyone was welcome to come. I told her I would be there; plus I wanted to see her boys play.

It was an all-day event. I got there around noon, and we sat in the bleachers and watched her son play. When the game had ended, she said, "Do you want to walk around and take a look at the auction items?"

I said, "Of course, that's one of the reasons I'm here!" And off we went to the area where they had set up the tents and tables. We hadn't been at the tables for more than a couple of minutes when I spotted a sign that said, "Photo session for a family of five." I looked at Lisa and said, "This is what I want." Then I explained to her what I wanted for my birthday, and there it was. No one had placed a bid yet, so I started the bidding with the minimum bid.

As I said before, the event was going on all day long, and I had to get back home. I said, "Lisa, please keep your eye on this. If anyone else places a bid, call me and I'll tell you my next bid. I will pay anything for this. After all, it's my fiftieth-birthday present, and this way the money is going to a good cause."

Hours passed and she called: someone had placed a higher bid. I told her to go ahead and place my bid twenty-five dollars higher than that one. There was still a lot of time left, and I said, "If anyone else bids, wait till there are only a couple of minutes left and place another bid for me twenty-five dollars higher."

After the auction had ended, she called and said, "It's yours!" I didn't think of it at the time, but how ironic that I got both of my family photo sessions through auctions that would benefit children.

I told my family we had to do the photo session sometime in October, when the weather was cooler in Florida, and in time to use one of the photos for our Christmas card. The day came, and my son was going to meet us, because he was living on his own, at the Boynton Inlet in Boynton Beach. As we were driving there, I said to my husband, "I sure hope Ryan is on time. I know he isn't crazy about getting his picture taken."

We arrived about fifteen minutes early. Within four minutes, Ryan appeared. Not only was he early, but he brought three different shirts so I could choose the one I liked best. I was overjoyed. It ended up being one of the best days I'd had in years. Our photos were taken in a nearby wooded area, on docks by the Intracoastal Waterway, and on the beach. It just happened that the photographer, Natasha Meyer, loved taking single shots of Ryan.[4] She captured my son in the most magnificent ways, better than I had ever been able to. Never could I have imagined that those terrific photos of him would become so important so soon and would be used in such a significant way—at his *celebration of life*.

I was so excited to select the perfect family picture that we would use for our Christmas card. I decided on one where we were all on the beach and we were really close together. We were so close, in fact, that all of our heads were almost touching one another. That's how I picture my family: close and always together.

Many years ago, my college roommate Chrissy had bought us a *Christmas Memories* book. When you open the book, on the left side is a place for your annual photo Christmas card, and on the right side is a place to write a few words about that Christmas. I had started the first year's section of the book with a picture of Ryan, our first-born, when he was only six days old. His birthday, as I mentioned earlier, was December 6.

As soon as I got the latest Christmas cards printed, I put one in the Christmas book. I don't write anything in it until Christmas is over. I did notice, when I put the photo on the left-hand page, that the page was blank. All the other pages had decorative borders on them.

After Ryan passed, some friends came to visit us. One of them noticed the Christmas book on the coffee table, and she picked it up and starting looking through it. I came over and sat next to her as she was thumbing through my Christmases past. When we got to that year's picture, she said, "This was the best of all your Christmas cards."

I immediately started to cry and said, "I can't believe it's my last one." Once I had collected myself, she also mentioned something about the page being blank. So she proceeded to flip to the next page to see if it was decorated, but there were no more pages. That year's Christmas card was on the last page of the book. The book began with the first Christmas picture of Ryan, and it ended with the last Christmas picture of him.

2014 Christmas photo
Meghan, Michael, Ryan, Linda, and Jaclyn

In preparation for the celebration, Michael thought it would be a great idea if our whole family wore DeMeco Ryans jerseys, just like the one I gave Ryan for his birthday. He called the Philadelphia Eagles NFL shop in Lincoln Financial Field and asked if they had the jerseys we wanted in our sizes. The woman at the shop said they had two of the five that we wanted on hand. Michael explained to her what had happened and what we wanted to do. She was so touched by our story that she said she would be able to get them printed up for us right away. We had some cousins who were flying down from Philly and would be able to pick up the jerseys and bring them to us in time for the celebration.

We were thrilled, so my husband went on social media and announced that the event was going to be a casual affair, and whoever owned an Eagles jersey should wear it, since that was what our whole family would be wearing and Ryan would have loved it.

Earlier that year, Ryan and my husband had decided to go to the Eagles versus the New York Giants game in Philadelphia. Michael and I were shocked when Ryan asked if he could bring his friend Shayla.

I knew she and Ryan had been close for at least three years, because her name kept coming up in conversations. But Shayla and her mother had recently moved to the west coast of Florida, which is a four-hour drive from where we lived. Ryan really wanted to take her because she was a Giants fan and had never been to a game. My husband and I were thrilled because Ryan had never brought a girl home, and I couldn't wait to meet someone he cared for this much. Michael agreed to order three tickets.

Ryan drove the four hours to pick Shayla up and four hours back to our house two days before the game because the next morning they were taking an early flight to Philly.

We had a wonderful night together. She was adorable, and I loved seeing how she behaved with him. The next morning the three of them flew to Philly for the game and had a wonderful time—and for the record, the Eagles won, 27–0.

After Ryan passed, Shayla called me and said that she and her mom, Diana, wanted to come to Ryan's celebration. Ryan had said several times that he couldn't wait for me to meet Diana because he thought we were very much alike. Without a second thought, I asked Shayla if they would like to stay at our house. I couldn't wait to meet Diana because I knew she had become very close to Ryan over the years. There was something about having them with me, two people who had been so close to Ryan, that made me feel closer to him. Their visit was wonderful for our family and for them. Sharing stories about Ryan was heartwarming.

Quattlebaum had also requested a list of Ryan's favorite songs, which would be playing in the background the whole evening. My husband's first request was "Fly Eagles Fly" the Philadelphia Eagles' fight song. I knew the type of music Ryan liked to a degree, but I had to reach out to his friends for a full playlist. They all came back with the song "Gold," by Adventure Club. Ryan loved the song so much he got the words "Stay Gold" tattooed over his heart. I later learned he did it because he believed he had a heart of gold.

Stay Gold

I called Shayla and asked her why he loved that song so much. She said, "Whenever we were sad or upset about something, we would always say, 'Stay gold,' meaning to 'stay strong.'" I listened to the song over and over and over again. At one point I felt the song was talking to me, that Ryan was telling me to "stay gold," to stay strong, because the next day was going to be one of the hardest I could ever imagine: the celebration of the life of my son.

One of the companies that Michael worked for had ordered us five hundred rubber bracelets that said "RIP Ryan" and "Fly Eagles Fly." We weren't sure if they would arrive on time. Jaclyn also ordered seventy bracelets that read "RIP Ryan" and "Gone but never forgotten." We were not sure if the "Fly Eagles Fly" bracelets would arrive in time for the celebration, but they did. Jaclyn's did not, but that actually worked out fine. Almost four hundred bracelets would be taken at the celebration, and Jaclyn's were saved for close family members and friends.

Christine and family

Chrissy and friends

Friday, December 19

———— ❧ ————

We arrived at Quattlebaum an hour before the celebration was to begin. As I crossed the threshold into the lobby, the first thing I saw was the digital marquee, with a striking picture of my son standing by the Atlantic Ocean, his full name across the bottom. That presentation was one of the first decisions I had made earlier. When Michael originally sent me a picture of the marquee, it had "1994–2014" beneath Ryan's name. I said, "I want the dates removed. They remind me of a funeral, and this is a celebration."

We were amazed at the transformation of what was a simply furnished and appointed room to one that was genuinely festive and inviting. My friends Patti, Rodger, Joan, and Diane had outdone themselves. The simple candle centerpieces had been transformed into beautiful bouquets of white flowers in greenery featuring miniature Eagles helmets. There were Eagles napkins, banners, and balloons. The plain white tablecloths had Eagles banners across them, and scattered across them were miniature pennants and pins. It was gorgeous. I imagined it was what a signing-day celebration room might look like. But this room was all to celebrate Ryan's life.

At one point during that evening, the owner, Greg Quattlebaum, came over to share a story, and once again the power of the Internet was evident. On his phone he had pulled up an article regarding a recent test launch at Kennedy Space Center in Cape Canaveral, just 140 miles north. NASA had finally succeeded in launching and re-trieving its new crew capsule designed for deep space missions, aptly named *Orion*, on December 5, 2014. The test had been plagued by technical glitches, causing mul-tiple delays, but the early morning launch—and capsule recovery—went off without a hitch on the day before Ryan's birthday.

It was somewhat strange that he shared this story with me, because until that night I had never met him. He said that the story had touched him because he had heard about my encounter with the constellation Orion. For me it was another affirmation that Ryan was reaching out to me in some awesome ways: constellations and rocket launches. But more importantly, he was working through some peo-ple in ways that were touching many people. Through all the heartache and sadness, these stories were real connec-tions for me, and for others, to Ryan.

The room decorated for the celebration looked fab-ulous, and as we were walking in, our funeral director, Richard, came up to us and said, "There is something special that I would like to show you." He walked us up to the front of the room, and beneath that huge portrait of Ryan was a magnificent floral arrangement. The card read:

Stay Gold

MacDonald Family,
We were saddened to learn about the passing of
a member of your family and fellow Eagles fan,
Ryan. We would like to present you with an of-
ficial game ball that was used in a game, to honor
Ryan's legacy. We hope that when you see this
game ball, it will help serve as a reminder of all
the great times you celebrated together. We view
the loss of Ryan as one of a family member and are
very appreciative that Ryan, as well as your family,
has cheered us on over the years.
Sincerely,
The Philadelphia Eagles

I was overwhelmed with emotion, and I fell to my knees,
sobbing. I couldn't believe what I was seeing. In a time
when national sports franchises had come to seem like
emotionless profit-oriented organizations, the Eagles had
taken the time to give so freely and caringly. What had
prompted them to be so kind? Was it the call from my husband about the Eagles Youth Partnership, or was it someone else? We still don't know, but I was sure that Ryan was
thrilled about it, and that made me smile.

Then the director led us to yet another magnificent
arrangement. It was made up of brilliant orchids in colors I had never seen before. I read the card, and it was
from the Philadelphia Eagles quarterback, Mark Sanchez.
At that point, I was in shock. I sat down to get my bear-
ings and just looked around the whole room. I looked at

all the flowers and the decorations and marveled at how it had all come together. Every detail was thought through, and every decision had been born of love and caring. I was amazed and overjoyed, for Ryan's sake.

We had anticipated that the day of the celebration, our whole family would stand together to greet people: Michael, Jaclyn, Meghan, and I. We assumed this based on all the other wakes and services we had attended. As people arrived, we were soon drawn apart into separate parts of the room. I was showing people to the photo boards, my labor of love, and then to the Eagles' flower wreath. Michael went to get a bottle of water but soon found himself stationed in the back of the room where the refreshments were set up, and he began speaking with his friends and coworkers. Jaclyn and Meghan seemed to be holding court in the middle of the room. It soon became a sea of young people, and there were smiles and laughter among the sad looks and tears of compassion. We all stayed in our separate stations throughout the entire time.

Jaclyn, my older daughter, was a high school senior at the time. She had been applying to colleges, mostly in Florida. She came to my husband and me one day and said, "Someone I know goes to the University of Alabama, and she loves it. I think I'm going to apply there." We said, "Great idea, go for it." On December 13, she got the acceptance letter from Alabama. She texted Ryan, telling him she had been accepted. He was so happy for her; he posted the text from her on Instagram and added: "I'm so proud of my sister!" That was his last post on Instagram. Jaclyn still wasn't sure she would go there; she wanted to wait to hear from the other colleges before deciding.

Danielle and Renee, my close friends and neighbors, were getting ready for the celebration at their home. They had agreed to let my college roommate Chrissy, who flew in from Atlanta, stay with them, since Shayla and her mom were staying with us. Chrissy asked, "Is Ryans a real player for the Eagles, or did they make the shirts up for Ryan?" None of them were sure, so Danielle, our Google queen, tried to find out. Sure enough, DeMeco Ryans was a real player.

As Danielle read further, she stopped and looked at Renee and Chrissy and said, "He went to the University of Alabama." They all were in shock because they knew Jaclyn had just been accepted there.

As soon as they got to Ryan's celebration, they came right up to us and said, "Did you know that DeMeco Ryans went to University of Alabama?"

I looked at my husband, thinking, *He knows so much about each player on the Eagles*, but he said, "No way, I had no idea." It's crazy because he was standing there wearing a jersey with the guy's name on the back!

As the celebration continued, I recalled that Quattlebaum had left me a captain's chair to collapse into if necessary—if not from the physical fatigue, then as an emotional time-out. Soon it became apparent from numerous comments like "I can't believe that you are even standing," "How are you functioning so well?," and "You have so much strength" that I was indeed handling it pretty well. And when I looked over my shoulder at the poster-sized picture of Ryan and his contagious smile, I knew he was the source of my strength. I knew then that I would get through that night and the celebration. I think he may have even winked at me. It was a defining moment, one of many that reassured me that Ryan was by my side and that I would survive this devastating event.

So many young people came to the celebration that it was clear the power of the Internet was at work. Some of them I knew, but many of them I didn't—but all of them were friends of our children.

Our children venture into the world as young adults and make friends, and we can ask about them but can never know them all. As our children grow up and become individuals, we strain to maintain our connection. We can see glimpses of their lives on Facebook and Instagram. We hear them talk to their siblings and hear snippets of recollections, but they are off forging their own courses in life. They go to school, they work and play, each one living his or her own life. We sneak them gas money, do their laundry, and snatch every opportunity to spend time with them, but they are their own beings; they are all pretty grown up.

Meeting Ryan's friends I hadn't met before allowed me another sneak peek into his life. The people that our children choose to get close to are a direct reflection of them. It seemed that all of them were taking selfies with Ryan's portrait, but they all reached out to me, too. Those I knew also gave me silent, warming hugs; many gave me several.

They stayed the whole time, lingering and comforting us and each other. Their love for Ryan was also a constant reminder that while he may not have had a physical presence, he was assuredly there. The fact that they too were grieving was not lost on me that day, or the following days, when some of them continued to come by to see how I was doing. I have some wonderful friends, and I think it is clear that in times of extreme adversity, they will perform acts of kindness that amaze and warm you.

I had not been rigorously attentive as a Catholic, and that made the task of finding a pastor to help us lead the celebration more daunting. However, once again, my friends came to the rescue. There was a much sought-after priest in our area, Father Brian King. He was a leader in the community and the right-hand man of the bishop of the Palm Beach diocese, Gerald Barbarito. Many of our friends asked him to preside, and at one point he commented on how truly wonderful the celebration was shaping up to be and that he would be happy to be a part of it.

Father Brian knew many of the people in the room and had the chance to visit with them and listen to all the stories being shared by Ryan's friends and family. The room was full of Ryan in so many ways: pictures, flowers, Eagles paraphernalia, people in Eagles jerseys, and all the Ryan stories. Father Brian knew that this was undoubtedly a celebration of life, not a sad send-off.

At the end of the celebration, people began to drift out the door. Many people lingered because they just needed to say a final something, or take one last look, or give someone another hug. It had lasted so much longer than I expected. In the beginning I thought that the time allotted, two hours, was excessive. How was I to get through those hours? But when it ended, over three hours later, I was left shaking my head and asking myself, *How did it pass so quickly?* Hundreds of people had come, the guest book was overflowing with names, and we could only imagine how many families had signed as one and how many young people had neglected to sign it at all.

Michael and I hung back. I stood for a while looking at the beautiful tables, decorations, pictures, and all the flower arrangements. I wanted to imprint the sight forever in my memory. The owner Greg and Richard were standing in the back with us. Michael and I thanked them for everything they had done to make this a true celebration. They both said, "We didn't do this. Both of you and your friends are the ones who made this celebration come to be what it was. We have never seen anything like this." Michael and I looked at each other and knew that we had created something that would affect everyone who was there for a long time and provide us with memories to take us through any darkness that lay ahead. We would have the memory of a gathering of people that took wings of its own and turned what could have been a melancholy event into a phenomenal celebration of our son's life.

After the celebration, we invited a few people back to our home. Most of them were from out of town. Shayla and her mother had driven separately because we didn't have enough room in our car. They arrived home first and were waiting out front. Shayla was extremely upset and just letting it all out with tears of anguish. She kept looking up at the sky and asking, "Please, Ryan, please send me a sign to let me know you are okay."

It was at that moment that they both looked down, and there were red rose petals scattered all over the ground by our front door. That miraculous wash of relief and acknowledgement came over them. Shayla knew that was her sign that Ryan was reaching out to soothe her broken heart. We asked everybody we knew who had left those flower petals there, but nobody took credit.

Saturday, December 20

THE DAY AFTER Ryan's celebration of life, Jaclyn said, "I want to go to the University of Alabama, and it doesn't matter what other colleges accept me." At that moment, I knew she had felt it was a sign from Ryan. Michael and Jaclyn had already signed up for a tour of the university in January. A couple of days after Ryan's celebration, Michael said, "I'm going to book you and Meghan on the trip to Alabama. It will be something we can do together since we know that's where Jaclyn wants to go."

Sunday, December 21

ON SUNDAY WE said our good-byes to family and friends who had flown in or driven here for the celebration. The number of people who had made the trip was staggering. Some were there longer than others, but each one had done his or her own part. How thankful and grateful my husband and I were to have them surround us with their love and support.

But after they left, it was almost too quiet. I was so used to people being around me, asking questions or just distracting me from my grief. Planning and preparing for the celebration were exactly what I had needed to get me motivated each day. Then it was all gone.

But soon it dawned on me: Christmas was in four days. It's my favorite time of year, and my daughters', too. I wondered how I could possibly do everything that needed to be done. My body ached from pure sadness. My body ached from pushing through every day to make the celebration a success. Both Jaclyn and Meghan had been so strong through all of this, too. I had just poured all of my strength into Ryan, but then I had to find the strength for my girls.

When I was a young, my mother was divorced, and I was an only child. I spent most of my time with my grandparents because my mother was always working. I adored them so much that I ended up calling my grandfather Dad and my grandmother Mom-Mom. My grandparents loved antiques, and the one toy I loved was an old-fashioned red cash register. My grandfather drank a lot of soda, and he would take out the round, plastic, disc-like insert from inside the bottles' screw-off caps. He would then take a piece of clear tape and place it in the center of the round plastic disc because it made it easier to write 1, 5, 10, or 25 on them to make them into play coins for my register. I still have that register in my office, but none of the old play coins.

Ryan's birthday was December 6, 1994. On December 2, 1995, my grandfather passed away, and on December 10, 1995, my grandmother passed away. Ryan had just had his first birthday. My grandfather had passed away suddenly from a ruptured ulcer. My grandmother was in hospice care for a while, and we knew she was going to pass away shortly. The funeral home was able to keep my grandfather until my grandmother passed away so we would be able to have a double funeral. I was overwhelmed with sadness then. But at the same time, I had a sense of peace. They had both lived full lives and were being laid to rest at the same time. Someone said, "It's like a love story. They were married for more than fifty years, and neither of them had to live alone."

First on my list of things to do to get ready for Christmas was to start wrapping presents. I started straightening up my room because that was where I liked to wrap. As I was vacuuming, I noticed something underneath a chair. The moment I saw it, I knew what it was, but

I couldn't believe it. I slowly walked over to the chair and bent down to pick it up. It was one of those toy coins my grandfather had made for me more than forty years earlier. I stared at it for the longest time, trying to understand how it could have gotten there. I hadn't seen any of those coins in over twenty years. As I stared at the coin, I noticed something very odd. There wasn't a 1, 5, 10, or 25 written on it. This one had "15" written on it. I ran downstairs to look at the drawer in the register to see if there were more than four slots in it for coins. I figured that if there were more than four slots, then maybe my grandfather had made an extra coin to fill a fifth slot. But there were only four. I looked at the coin again, and something came to me: Ryan had died on the fifteenth. I truly believe it was a sign from Ryan that he was with my grandparents.

Monday, December 22

———— ❧ ————

I FOUND MYSELF SPENDING hours sitting outside, looking around, both day and night. Orion kept me company at night, and during the day the stillness of the lake helped soothe my racing mind.

One day I noticed a bird sitting in a tree directly in front of me. I took solace in the bird's natural grace and stillness. I sat on the wicker love seat that Ryan had always used, and as the day went on, I realized that the same bird was still there, in the same place. That was pretty unusual. At first I was just in awe of this bird's tenacity, sitting still for so very long, on the smallest of branches, which would sway back and forth with the wind. Then night came, and the bird was still there. I had told my family earlier in the day about the bird, and as time passed, each one of them, at different times, had poked his or her head out to see if the bird was still there, and it was. It gave me such a peaceful feeling, like it was watching over me. Shortly before ten o'clock, I was feeling exhausted, but I didn't want to leave the bird. It hadn't left me all day and night, and I felt bad leaving it, but I went to bed. The bird returned every day after that. I never saw it feed from the lake and didn't see a nest, so why did this bird keep coming back to keep me company?

I found sharing these stories with my friends to be healing. As I was relating this story to my friend Tina, she shared that she believed that the spirits of people who have died come back in animals for a time. She said, "The bird may not always be there, but it will be there when you are in need." I had heard many stories about how butterflies have such meaning to people who have lost someone. Our family's fondness for birds comes from our love for the Philadelphia Eagles, sometimes referred to as "the Birds." It made sense that Ryan would again reach out through a bird to make a connection. "Fly Eagles Fly" became a phrase that had deeper meaning for us.

Stay Gold

Thursday, January 1

———— ❧ ————

IT WAS NEW Year's Day, a new year. My husband woke up, came downstairs, and poured himself a cup of coffee. He looked over at me and said, "Did you ever notice the numbers of the year? It's twenty fifteen. Ryan was twenty, and he died on the fifteenth."

I shook my head and started to cry. It was weird because every time someone would reference the new year, they never said "two thousand and fifteen." They would just say "twenty fifteen." To many of you, it may look like we were trying to make something out of this, but we were not.

My friend Rodger, the one who helped with the decorations for the celebration, said that he was very much into numbers. He made many connections with numbers. He gave me an example: "There was a picture at the celebration with Michael and Ryan at an Eagles game. Ryan was wearing a jersey with the number twenty-two on it, and Michael was wearing a jersey with the number seven on it. If you subtract them, it equals fifteen, the day Ryan passed."

I looked at Rodger and said, "Wow, I can't believe that's what you got out of that picture. Is that the way you look at a lot of things, by the numbers?"

He said, "Hell, yeah, it's all about the numbers!" I sat there in amazement, trying to process all of it. I remembered there was a television show called *Numb3rs*. I had watched it a few times, and I found it fascinating. There was another picture of Ryan with his Eagles jersey on displayed at the celebration. It was taken at the first Eagles game he attended with his dad, and his jersey had the number twenty on it, the age of his passing.

Michael's sister was another person who was into numbers. She played the "Play 4" Florida lottery game every day. She felt very strongly about playing numbers with a connection to Ryan. One morning she decided to play 1215, December 15, the day he passed. Unfortunately, the number did not come up in the morning, but it did come up for the second drawing that night. On another day she decided to play 1294, December 1994, for Ryan's birthday, and she won that time. Her coworker had put a dollar on 1994, the year Ryan was born, and won $200.

Tuesday, January 6

AFTER RYAN PASSED, I knew I wanted to get another tattoo. It was mind-blowing how many kids had already gotten tattoos in remembrance of Ryan. The majority of them were huge in size: angels, quotations, flowers, "Fly Eagles Fly," his full name with dates underneath. Thinking back to when I was putting together the playlist of songs for his celebration, "Gold" kept coming to mind—how I felt he was telling me to stay gold, stay strong through the celebration.

After losing a child, you realize that your life will never be the same, that you will always have that sadness deep inside of you, that a piece of you is gone. Thinking that Ryan was trying to tell me to "stay gold" for the celebration was only the beginning. I was going to have to stay gold for the rest of my life. That's when I knew what my tattoo would be. Just like he inspired me for my first tattoo, he inspired me for my last one, which of course reads "Stay Gold."

I was so excited about my decision that I ran to tell my family and Danielle and Renee, who were with me for my first tattoo. Jaclyn said to me, "Mom, I want to go with you and get another tattoo for Ryan. I even know what I'm going to get."

I looked at her in shock, not just because she wanted another one but because she had put that much thought into it and knew what she wanted. I said, "Oh, Jac, why?"

She replied, "I knew I wanted to get another one for Ryan, and I found the perfect one. It's three black birds in a row, flying." Three has always represented the number of kids in our family, and the bird reminded her of the bird we had outside watching over us. Then there were the Eagles, alias "the Birds." Then she said, "Plus this will be the mother-daughter tattooing we never got to do before."

That all made sense to me, so I said, "Okay."

When Danielle and Renee got wind of it, they wanted to go too. Then my other daughter, Meghan, who was fifteen, wanted one too. I put my foot down on that one and said, "You are going to have to wait till you're seventeen."

Then she said, "Well, can I get my cartilage pierced? Plus it will be something the three of us get to do together." It was something she had been wanting awhile, so I said yes.

The five of us got to the tattoo parlor around five, and there were no other customers. So Jaclyn and I were able to get our tattoos done at the same time. Danielle, Renee, and Meghan floated back and forth between us to keep us company. By the time the tattoo artists were finishing up our tattoos, another one had started piercing Meghan's cartilage. We all stood around and kept her company. It was the perfect night, one we will never forget. Each one of us got something in remembrance of Ryan. And the date was the sixth; Ryan was born on the sixth.

Wednesday, January 7

THE ONE THING we were told by several people was that everyone grieves differently. I also believe we all can be consoled differently. It's not that my husband or I are any sadder than the other; we just show it differently and at different times.

Here is a story from my husband, Michael:

I was making my first business trip since Ryan's death. I was on my way to the Atlanta Gift Show for a week. I have my own company, and I am an independent sales representative. I sell for many manufacturers to multiple national retailers like Bed Bath & Beyond and Ross Stores. So this meant I would be meeting with many business partners during the week of the show. It would be the first time I had seen them since Ryan passed. I was very nervous and did not know what to expect. I knew it would be a long week, and I would have to try to keep a happy face during all those meetings.

When I arrived at the show, so many people came up to me, hugged me, and gave me their sincere condolences. It was very touching, and it warmed my heart. During the show I had an experience that really touched me. I ran into a woman I had worked with years ago. I was her boss back in the late 1990s when I worked for a manufacturer.

She was working in the hallway with her company. As I walked down the hallway, I recognized her, and something lured me over to stop and speak with her. I was not sure if she would remember me, but she did instantly. During the show I had not really brought up Ryan or his death to anyone. The people who had approached me at the show knew about Ryan's death only because of social media. She asked me how I was doing, and for some reason I decided to tell her what happened to Ryan. When I was done, I was surprised at her response. She told me that she had three children like me. She had two daughters and a son, just like me. Her son was the oldest, once again, just like me. She then proceeded to tell me she had lost her son at the same age as Ryan, twenty years old, just like me. I asked her what happened, and she told me that her son had problems with seizures, and when he was twenty years old, he had a very bad seizure and was taken to the hospital. She was traveling that day and rushed home to be with her son at the hospital. Unfortunately, by the time she arrived, her son had died. I gave her my condolences. I had never known about the death of her son and what she had gone through, but I instantly knew she felt my pain and I felt hers.

She continued to tell me a very inspirational story. She said that after her son's death, she had a very hard time getting up every day and continuing with life. She still had two beautiful daughters she needed to care for. One day she was driving on the highway to do a retail store setup.

As she was driving, she started to contemplate taking her own life so she could be with her son again. She thought about just crashing her car. Then she heard a voice telling her to pull off the highway. She decided to get a cup of coffee to calm down. She spent a few minutes getting the coffee and then proceeded on her way. As she was driving back onto the highway, she saw that traffic was backed up, and she came upon a major accident and a huge pileup of cars. To that day, she told me, she believed the voice she heard was her son's. He was the one who told her to pull over. She also believed that if she had not pulled over, she would have been in that major accident. From that point forward, she decided to live life to the fullest and live life for her son. She went on to raise her daughters and live a very productive life. She missed her son but credited him for all that she had achieved in her life.

The story that she told me that day and all the signs that Linda and I had been receiving from Ryan since his death made me realize we must move on and live life. We would love and miss Ryan every day, but he would want us to lead a productive, loving life with his sisters, our daughters. I thank God every day that I ran into her that day and she shared her story. It not only inspired me, but it made me realize that you really never know the burden or pain many other families go through. It's always important to remember this and treat others the way you would want to be treated.

I had one other experience while I was at the Atlanta Gift Show. It was a simple but touching moment. It was day three of the show, and I decided to go to dinner with a few friends. We went to a great burger place in Midtown Atlanta called the Vortex. While we were getting close to the restaurant, we started searching for a parking lot. We found one and decided to pull in. It was one of those lots where you park and then buy your ticket at a ticket machine. As I was approaching the machine, I ran into a homeless man in his late sixties. As I approached the ticket machine, he asked me if I could give him some money for food. I said absolutely and asked him to give me a minute while I got my parking ticket. When I turned around to give him some money, I noticed he was wearing a football jacket. I could not believe it, but it was a Philadelphia Eagles jacket.

At that moment I thought, *What are the odds that a guy from Atlanta would be an Eagles fan?* I asked him about the jacket, and he said he loved the Eagles. I was touched because Ryan and I were avid Eagles fans. I had brought Ryan to Philadelphia Eagles football games every year from the time he was ten until the age of twenty. It was always a special weekend for us and a time to just relax and enjoy an Eagles home game with all the Philadelphia fans. We would always plan our next trip right after we attended the game. We would talk about it all year until we got to that next game. We debated which team we should see them play. Should we go when it was still somewhat warm or when it got cold? This was always a big consideration because both of us, being Floridian boys, had to always consider the temperature.

Stay Gold

Seeing that Philadelphia Eagles football jacket on the homeless man made me smile. It made me realize that in some small way, Ryan was trying to give me a sign and was saying, "Dad, it's okay, it's okay, and please just remember all those great memories we had at all the Philadelphia Eagles games." I handed the homeless man some money, wished him well, told him, "God bless you," and smiled.

Sunday, January 11

Every Sunday during football season, we order takeout, usually with Danielle and Renee, our neighbors. None of us feel like cooking or cleaning up the kitchen because Sundays are all about watching football. On that Sunday we decided on Fratelli's Restaurant & Pizzeria.

When the order arrived, I went outside to pay the delivery guy, and he said, "Don't worry about it. It's been taken care of."

I said, "What do you mean?" and he handed me a piece of paper with five names on it. I looked at the names and said, "I don't know any of these people."

He said, "You did lose your son recently, didn't you?"

Tears started streaming down my cheeks, and I could barely get the word out. "Yes," I said softly.

He replied, "Please don't worry about it. Your dinner has been taken care of."

I gave him a twenty-dollar tip, took the food, and went back into the house. My husband looked at me and asked, "What's wrong?"

The tears were still streaming down my cheeks, and with a shaky voice I said, "Our dinner has been taken care of."

Michael asked me what I meant, and I handed him the piece of paper and informed him that these strangers had paid for our dinner. He looked at the piece of paper and said, "All these girls grew up with me in Pennsylvania. But they all still live there. How could this happen?" So, perplexed by it all, he reached out to them right away via Facebook.

He got a hold of one of them, and she said, "We wanted to do something for you and your family, and we thought dinner being delivered was a good idea." Michael thanked her and asked what had made her order from that particular restaurant. She explained how they had Googled restaurants near our house that delivered, and that one had sounded perfect. When she called Fratelli's, she explained that she was from Pennsylvania and wanted to have food delivered to a family that had just lost their son. She gave the guy our name and address to make sure that the restaurant delivered to our neighborhood, and he put her on hold and checked. When he came back on the phone, he told her that yes, they did deliver there, but the odd thing was that the name seemed so familiar. So he went to check on the previous orders that had been placed, and sure enough, we had placed an order only fifteen minutes before she called. She was stunned and relieved because she no longer would have to guess what we might want. We had already placed the order!

So it was another one of those unusual coincidences. There are dozens of restaurants around us the women could have chosen. Of all the days they decide to order for us, it was the day that we ordered takeout from the same place, and they made the call only moments after I called. It's one of those times when most people would say, "Unbelievable." But not me. I think of Ryan and smile to myself.

Thursday, January 15

MICHAEL AND I had planned a trip to Charleston, North Carolina, to see one of my college roommates, Kimmie, and her husband. They always come to see us here in Florida to escape the cold, but that year it was our turn to go see them. But with all that had transpired, we canceled the trip. Kimmie called me one day and said she had a business meeting in Fort Lauderdale and wanted to know if she could come by and visit me. I told her I thought it would be a better idea if I came to see her; it would get me out of the house.

I met her at her hotel, which was on the beach, and she said our room wasn't ready yet. There was a cute restaurant across the street, right on the water, so we decided to have lunch while we waited for the room to be cleaned. When we got there, it was packed. There was a forty-minute wait. The hostess gave us a buzzer that would go off when our table was ready, so we started to walk outside to wait, and the buzzer went off.

Kimmie said, "That must be a mistake."

I shook my head and said, "No, it's not. I'll explain later." I was, of course, thinking of Ryan. So many crazy things had been happening that this latest one did not surprise me in the least.

We went back in to the hostess stand and were told our table was ready. We sat outside by the water, talking for hours. I shared all of my stories with her, from the Orion constellation to the bird, the coin, Shayla's rose petals, all the numbers—everything. When I brought up the buzzer, she laughed and said, "Now I get it. It must be Ryan."

We decided we wanted to sit on the beach. It was a beautiful day. After a while, we figured that by that time, the room should be ready. So we walked back over to the hotel, and it was ready. The desk clerk handed us our keys and said, "You're in room 920." (There's that twenty again, Ryan's age.) We looked at each other and shook our heads.

Kimmie said, "Linda, this is crazy. But I so believe he just wants to keep reminding you that he is always with you." I smiled and looked at her and said, "I think you're right. And I'm so glad you got to witness it yourself."

On that day it had been exactly one month since Ryan passed away. The number fifteen will always have a deep meaning to me. So it didn't surprise me that Ryan would send out signs that day—not only so Kimmie could witness it but for me as well. Even when I was away from my home, he was still with me.

Wednesday, January 21

❧

HERE IS ANOTHER story from my husband, Michael:

It had been several weeks since Ryan passed away. I was having a really hard week dealing with my sadness, and I decided to do something to help ease the pain. I had been referred by a very close friend named Charlie to a group called The Compassionate Friends.[5] Charlie had a close friend who had lost a child, and she suggested strongly that I could benefit from attending a meeting to gain some peace of mind. The Compassionate Friends is a national group that has many regional and community meetings. It was founded and is run by parents who have lost a child of any age.

As I drove to my first meeting, I was very nervous. I attended the meeting by myself because Linda was not ready to be in a group setting. It was much too early for her. I completely understood, and I told her I would attend and let her know how it went. As I entered the meeting room, I saw there were several people, and I did not know what to expect. I took my seat, and the meeting started.

Each person or couple in the room told their story. When it was my turn I explained how Ryan had died just five weeks earlier. I cried as I told my story, and it was very sad. But after I spoke about Ryan and what happened, I felt a sense of release or relief. I felt for the first time since Ryan died that I was around people who really knew how I felt and how overwhelmingly sad I was. It was a sadness I had never experienced before, a sadness I could never explain to my friends and family members who had never lost a child. It was a sadness that I knew Linda clearly understood, but this was the first time I knew that others knew our pain as well.

As the people around me shared stories about the child they had lost, I saw in their eyes and heard in their voices the same pain and sadness I felt. Once every story was told, we had several discussions. There were many questions I wanted to ask to find out if the things I had been thinking about were normal. This was my first meeting, and I wanted to pose these questions to the people who had lost a child and for whom some time had passed.

Every day I thought about Ryan. I saw so many things that reminded me of him during the day, and it was consuming me. I loved thinking about and remembering all the great times with Ryan, but it also made me sad sometimes, and I would find myself crying. I wanted to know if this would ever get better and when I would stop crying. Would my pain lessen?

The group leader responded to my questions. She said, "Mike, it will never stop. You will think about Ryan every day for the rest of your life. It will get easier, but it will never stop. This will become your new normal. Nothing will be normal again for anyone in this room. We have all lost a child, so life will never be normal again. So please know you now have a new normal, and this new normal will involve your thinking of Ryan every day. This is okay, and his memories will bring you more peace than sadness as time passes."

At that moment I started to understand. I had a few other questions throughout the meeting, and I listened as others responded or posed questions of their own. As the meeting was winding down, one of the group leaders started to talk about the Angel of Hope. He had made mention of it a few times during the meeting. I was not really sure what he was talking about, and the woman next to me seemed to notice my confusion. She raised her hand and asked our group leader to explain what the Angel of Hope was for the benefit of the new people at the meeting.

The group leader, Ken, explained that the Angel of Hope is a statue that is erected in many cemeteries in remembrance of all the parents who have lost children. He went on to explain it originated in a book called *The Christmas Box*, by Richard Paul Evans. I had never read the book, and I had never heard about the Angel of Hope statue. I just thought at that moment that it was such a great tribute to parents who had lost their child or children. Little did I know, at that moment, how *The Christmas Box* would change my life.

I had spent several hours in the meeting, and it had come to a close. I had experienced sadness and joy during the meeting, but I was so glad I attended, and I knew I would be back. It really brought me a sense of peace and definitely a better understanding of what I was experiencing.

On my drive home, I called Linda and filled her in on The Compassionate Friends meeting. I told her of my experiences and about several discussions we'd had at the meeting and how it had helped me a great deal. For some reason I totally forgot to tell her about the Angel of Hope. When I arrived home, Linda and I discussed other topics, and she mentioned that she really wanted me to start to write about some of my experiences since Ryan's passing for the book she wanted to write.

I told her that I just wasn't ready yet. I also asked her why she was in such a rush, and I said there was no way she had written enough pages yet to complete a full book. Linda said, "While I was cleaning out the garage today, I found something." She walked into her office and came back into the kitchen and handed me a book. It was a very thin book, and Linda explained that she did not want to write a lengthy book but rather wanted one about that size. My eyes lit up because the book she handed me was *The Christmas Box*. I was shocked.

Linda looked at me and said, "What's wrong?"

I said, "You're not going to believe it, but we discussed this book at The Compassionate Friends meeting tonight!" I started to tell her about the Angel of Hope. I opened the book, and in it was a handwritten note from Linda's friend Shelley, dated December 1997. Shelley had written: "Linda, I thought you would enjoy this wonderful story. Merry Christmas. Love, Shelley."

Stay Gold

I decided to look in the book to see if there was a description of the Angel of Hope. I looked in the back of the book first, and I saw the "In Memoriam" page. I started to read the page out loud, and it went as follows:

In Memoriam

The Angel statue, of which the author makes mention, was destroyed in 1984 by the great floods that came through the Salt Lake Valley.

A new Angel monument, in remembrance of all those who have lost children, is being erected in the same Salt Lake City cemetery and it will be dedicated December 6, 1994.

The author wishes to invite all those who find themselves in Salt Lake City to lay a white flower at the statue's base.

As I read the dedication date, my jaw dropped. I looked at Linda and said, "December 6, 1994, the day Ryan was born." I was feeling goose bumps. How strange it was that I had never heard of the Angel of Hope statue or *The Christmas Box* until that day at The Compassionate Friends meeting, and that I had not mentioned any of this to Linda after the meeting. And she just happened to just clean out the garage that day and find *The Christmas Box* book given to her many years ago, and then give it to me merely to reference the thickness of the book she wanted to write. And lastly, the memoriam page referenced the day Ryan was born.

This could not all have been a coincidence. I thought, *No way could all these things just happen to come together on the same day.* I looked at Linda and said, "Ryan is reaching out to us. I think he knew how sad I was at the meeting tonight. I think he is trying to say, 'Dad, it's okay. I'm safe. Don't worry. I am okay.'" Linda and I both felt a great sense of peace at that moment.

Friday, January 23

THIS WAS THE day that Michael, Jaclyn, Meghan, and I were going to Tuscaloosa to visit the University of Alabama. Michael and I couldn't wait to get away and focus on something happy. It had been so hard, and we had been so sad; we couldn't stop thinking of Ryan. But we knew that we were not going to let our girls down and would always be there for them.

We got off the plane and headed toward the car rental agencies. Michael went to get the car key, and when he came out, he said our rental car was in slot B-20. I smiled and said, "There's the number twenty again." As I mentioned before, that number reminded me of Ryan because that's how old he was when he passed. And it was the date of my birthday, too. My family smiled at me, but they weren't feeling it like I was.

We headed to the hotel to check in. We got our key, and we were in room 120. I looked at my family and didn't say a word. Jaclyn looked at me and said, "Okay, now this is crazy." I smiled to myself because I knew they got it and didn't think I was crazy.

We arrived late in the afternoon, and our tour wasn't until the next day, so we just drove around the campus to get a feel for it. It was gorgeous. Every building was made of brick, which I was so used to from when I lived up north. The campus was so clean. The football stadium was magnificent. We kept driving around the campus, not knowing everything we were seeing but liking all that we saw.

When it started to get dark, we were starving. So we drove around outside of the campus to see where we might stop and eat. As we drove, we passed a restaurant with bright lights called Ryan's. We all noticed it, looked at each other, and said, "Wow. That's crazy." We drove a little further, and there was a restaurant called Philly's. We all agreed that this was too much and laughed because we were in Alabama, so why was there a restaurant called Philly's? We ended up at a Cheddar's and had a great dinner.

Restaurants near the University of Alabama

I couldn't sleep that night. I kept thinking of Jaclyn, how excited she was to go to the University of Alabama, and then thought how much I would miss her. Then I thought about Ryan and how much I missed him. I think it was a little after five in the morning, and I couldn't lie there anymore. So I got up, got dressed, and went to the lobby to get some coffee. I sat there and drank my coffee. I didn't want to go back to the room because I didn't want to wake anyone up. I was so sad. There we were, on this trip for Jaclyn, and I was thinking of Ryan more than ever. Between the number twenty and the restaurants, why was this happening? I decided to text my friend Kimmie because I knew she would get a kick out of our room number. I had stayed in two different hotels in one month, and both room numbers had ended in twenty. I knew it was early, and it was a Saturday morning, but it made me feel good to just reach out to her. To my surprise, she replied right away. We decided to talk instead of text. Soon we were laughing about how both of us were up so early on a Saturday morning, and neither of us had anyone to talk to until then. I filled her in on the number thing and the restaurants. She was not surprised by any of it. I said to her, with tears streaming down my face, "I just don't understand why all these things are happening. We came here to focus on Jaclyn, and I'm being reminded, even more than usual, of Ryan."

She said, "Linda, this is Ryan's way of letting you know this is the perfect place for Jaclyn. If you had any doubts in your mind about the college, he's trying to tell you this is where she should be. I also think he wants you to know that no matter where you are, he is always with you."

I was silent, trying to process everything she had said. I took a deep breath and said, "I think you're right. Now it all makes sense." That was true, even down to the fact that she was available to talk to me when I really needed to hear a friend's voice. With a new attitude, I was ready to face the day.

The tour was awesome. Our guide was outstanding. We loved everything we saw, and we learned so much about the university. The tour ended at the infamous bell tower, which is across the street from the president's house. Around the bell tower are concrete blocks with each of the football captains' names from all the years past. My family and I walked around the bell tower looking at the names of all the previous captains. They had a block with Joe Namath's name on it. I hadn't known he went to Alabama.

Then my husband called my name. I walked over to him, and he said, "Look at this one." I looked down, and it was DeMeco Ryans, 2005. Yes, we did know that he had gone to school there, but he hadn't been on my mind as we walked around the bell tower. I smiled, thought of what Kimmie had said earlier, and knew deep in my heart that this was the place for Jaclyn, and yes, I knew Ryan was always with me.

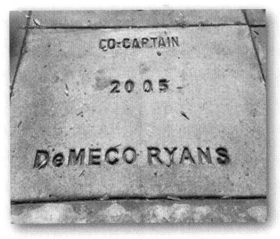

Demeco Ryans name on the Alabama
football captains walk of fame.

The University of Alabama's Denny Chimes Bell Tower

Friday, January 30

Two DAYS BEFORE Super Bowl Sunday, I had to go to Quattlebaum to pick up three necklaces that they had made for us. They were sterling silver with an oval disc hanging from the chain, and in the center of the disc was Ryan's fingerprint. They were for each of my daughters and me. They were beautiful, such a unique idea. Quattlebaum had also given me a memory book that they had made with all the pictures I had sent in for the television slide show. On the front cover was the striking picture of Ryan that had been displayed on the marquee by the entrance to his celebration. Along with the photos were a number of quotations, sayings, and poems.

When I got home, I couldn't wait to put the necklace on. I ran to look at it in the mirror, and it was perfect. Then I walked back into the kitchen and looked down at the memory book. I picked it up and walked into the dining room and laid it down on the dining room table. I was not ready to look at it. It's so odd that there were some things I had no problem with and there were others I was just not ready for. The memory book was one of those things I was not ready for.

Sunday, February 1

WE HAD NOT made any special plans for Super Bowl Sunday. Our team wasn't playing, we really weren't in the mood for any kind of party, and we just weren't comfortable being in a crowd. How depressing. I love football, I love making appetizers, and I love having friends over. But not for that Super Bowl. Everything was different for that one. We knew that we were going to have our good days and our bad days, and *that* Sunday was not a good one for me. I couldn't believe Ryan wasn't there. I couldn't believe he was not going to be watching the Super Bowl. I couldn't believe that I couldn't pick up a phone and call him. I couldn't believe I wouldn't be getting any more texts from him.

As I mentioned before, my husband and I handle things differently, and we felt differently about this. That Super Bowl Sunday morning, Michael went right over to the dining room table, sat down, and started leafing through the memory book. He called me in to show me something. I took a deep breath because I really was not in the mood to look through it yet. He showed me the first page, which read:

"We are tied to the ocean. And when we go back to the sea, whether it is to sail or to watch—we are going back from whence we came."—John F. Kennedy

We looked at each other and thought about the words.

Several weeks earlier we had chartered a gorgeous boat to take the four of us out into the ocean, near Boynton Inlet, to release Ryan's ashes. It was the perfect place because, as I mentioned before, one of the best days I'd had in years was when we did the family photo shoot there. I had also learned that the last day Ryan was alive, he went to the Boynton Inlet. So when Michael read me the quote from John F. Kennedy, it made us think of Ryan, and then we felt tied to the ocean because of him.

That night the Super Bowl came on, and Michael and I watched it. Of course, the game is not the only thing we find interesting; we also love the commercials. And early in the game, a commercial came on with a picture of the ocean and a narrator speaking in the background. It was John F. Kennedy's voice, and what did he say? His words were those on the first page of Ryan's memory book, which we had read just that morning. The commercial was for Carnival Cruise Lines, whose ship we had booked passage on in six weeks. Ryan was supposed to go with us.

It was not like I was looking for signs, but when things happened on the same day, it seemed like more than just coincidence. My husband and I once again felt as though Ryan was reaching out to us, letting us know he was watching the game or maybe just giving us a reminder that he was with us. It seemed especially true when I was having a very sad day. When something like that happened, it made me smile. It eased the pain, just a little.

All the events that I have shared with you took place in the first six weeks of Ryan's passing, starting with the first day. Six weeks of the darkest and saddest time of my life. But each and every one of these moments is what has helped me get through each day. Some are big and some small, but I can only hope one of these stories may help just one person with his or her own loss.

I have always been a person who liked to do things on my own. I was never comfortable asking for help, until now. By allowing myself to accept others' help, it not only benefited me, but it also gave them a sense of peace that there was something they could do for someone in the darkest days of her life. Ryan's celebration would have never been what it was without the help of my friends. The friends and family who had visited when I wasn't sure I wanted people over comforted me.

From day one of Ryan's passing, my husband was amazing with the words and articles he posted on Facebook. He was the one who got the word out about dressing down for the celebration and wearing Eagles jerseys. Many people went out and bought Eagles jerseys. Someone said he went to buy one but all the store had left was T-shirts; there were no more Eagles jerseys left in Palm Beach County. Michael is also the one who reached out to inform everyone about making donations to the Eagles Youth Foundation in lieu of flowers. The foundation got back to us and informed us that thousands of dollars had been donated in Ryan's name.

For Ryan's celebration, my husband wrote a eulogy. No matter how painful or difficult it would be, he knew he had to do this. He wanted to do this. He kept saying, "I'm going to write it today," but something would come up, and he wasn't able to write it. Then came the day of the celebration. He said he needed to leave the house to clear his head, so he headed to the library. Before he left, he said, "I'm still not sure what I'm writing."

I said, "I know something will happen to inspire you." Here is part of Michael's eulogy:

> *I want to share a story with you all. I waited until to-day to write these words because I didn't know what to write. I decided to go to the library so I could gather my thoughts. As I approached the library, I saw a young man about Ryan's age sitting on a bench, and he looked so sad. I have never done this before, but I approached him and asked him what was wrong. He said he and his father lost their house, and they were homeless. He was tired and was trying to rest on the bench. I decided to tell him about Ryan. I told him no matter what, things will get better, and there are always people out there to help him. His father came out of the library, and I gave them money to get a hotel room. I wanted them to get some rest. They did not want to take the money, because they were too proud. I insisted. They thanked me so much,*

and I knew it was Ryan in my heart and soul guiding me to approach this young man. Ryan, I want to thank you for leading me down the path to help others.

When I was sharing some of my amazing experiences with my friend Tina, she said, "You need to write all these things down." I knew some of these things had touched her, for she still has pain from the loss of her mother and brother. Then she said, "Honestly, you should write a book." At that moment, I knew I would. I could finally put my thoughts, feelings, and experiences into words, just like my husband had from day one. Ryan's words were ringing in my head: "I will leave an echo in this world that will last forever." A book will last forever, and so will his echo.

I truly believe that by sharing these experiences with others, I can help them with their own losses. So, Ryan, I also would like to thank you for leading me down the path to help others.

I have stayed in touch with several of Ryan's friends. Troy reached out to me and asked if I had a wooden rosary. He got the rosary when he was a kid and had given it to Ryan. I told him I did have it, and if he wanted to meet me at Boynton Inlet, I could give it back to him. I got to Boynton Inlet early and decided to take some pictures. It was the beach where we did our family photos and also where we released Ryan's ashes. It was such a beautiful day. Shortly after I finished taking some pictures, Troy, Justin, and Kyle showed up. I gave Troy back his rosary, and the four of us started telling stories of how some crazy things were happening to all of us. I shared some of my stories, and they all agreed that they could feel that Ryan was all around, that he was there with us on the beach, smiling down on us. It felt so good to see those boys and share stories with them. It made me think of Father Brian the night of the celebration, saying, "This celebration has been a beautiful thing. People coming together, sharing their stories and feelings about Ryan. Don't let it stop after tonight. Keep getting together, and share your stories." Troy mentioned that he had never really believed in spiritual things, but now he did. It reminded me of Grace saying the same thing. She hadn't really believed in signs, but after some of the things that had happened to her, she had a change of heart.

When I got home, I started looking through the pictures that I had taken on the beach. One of the pictures really stood out. There was something odd about it. As I stared at it, I noticed something in the ocean splash to the left of a wave crashing. It was a silhouette of an angel. I sent the picture to a few of my friends, and indeed, they could see it too. So the boys were right. Ryan was with us that day on the beach.

To all of those who have lost someone, stay gold. Open your heart to signs from them. I truly believe they will be there.

Angel silhouette in photo taken at the Boynton Inlet

Ryan Patrick MacDonald at Boynton Inlet—Stay Gold

Notes

1. Star Date. "Orion, the Hunter." 15 Dec. 2014.
   <http://stardate.org/nightsky/constellations/orion>

2. Quattlebaum Funeral, Cremation, and Event Center.
   16 Dec. 2014.
   <http://www.dignitymemorial.com/quattlebaum-
   funeral-cremation-and-event-center/en-us/index.
   page>

3. Philadelphia Eagles Youth Partnership. 17 Dec. 2014.
   <http://www.philadelphiaeagles.com/community/
   eagles-youth-partnership.html>

4. Tasharazzi Photography. Oct. 2014.
   <http://tasharazziphotography.com>

5. The Compassionate Friends. 15 Dec. 2014.
   <https://www.compassionatefriends.org/home.aspx>

Made in the USA
San Bernardino, CA
04 March 2017